History and Activities of the

Aztecs

Lisa Klobuchar

Heinemann Library
Chicago, Illinois

Designed by Kimberly R. Miracle in collaboration with Cavedweller Studio
Originated by Chroma Graphics
Printed in China by WKT Company Limited

11 10 09 08 07
10 9 8 7 6 5 4 3 2 1

The Library of Congress has cataloged the first edition as follows:
Klobuchar, Lisa.
        History and activities of the Aztecs / Lisa Klobuchar.
               p. cm. -- (Hands-on ancient history)
        Includes bibliographical references and index.
        ISBN 1-4034-7921-6 (HC) -- ISBN 1-4034-7929-1 (PB)
        1. Aztecs--History--Juvenile literature.
        2. Aztecs--Social life and customs--Juvenile literature.
        I. Title. II. Series.

F1219.73.K56 2007
972'.01--dc22   2005035173
13-digit ISBNs:
978-1-4034-7921-1 (hardcover)
978-1-4034-7929-7 (paperback)

Acknowledgments
The author and publishers are grateful to the following for permission to reproduce
photographs: Alamy Images, pp. **15** (Mireille Vautier), **17** (Rob Bartee); Ancient Art
and Architecture Collection, p. **7** (C M Dixon); Art Directors and Trip, pp. **8** (Helene
Rogers), **16** (University Of Essex), **26** (The University of Essex); Art Resource NY, pp. **10**
(Werner Forman), **12** (Werner Forman), **9** (SEF); Bridgeman Art Library, pp. **4** (Stapleton
Collection), **18** (Private Collection, Boltin Picture Library); Corbis, pp. **5** (Bettmann), **11**
(Gianni Dagli Orti), **13** (Kevin Schafer), **22** (Werner Forman); Harcourt, pp. **21** (David
Rigg), **25** (David Rigg), **29** (David Rigg); Mexicolore, p. **14**.

Cover photographs of a man wearing a green Aztec headdress (foreground) reproduced
with permission of Alamy Images (Felix Stensson) and the holy city of Teotihuacan
(background) reproduced with permission of Getty Images.

The publishers would like to thank Eric Utech for his assistance in the preparation of
this book.

Every effort has been made to contact copyright holders of any material reproduced in
this book. Any omissions will be rectified in subsequent printings if notice is given to the
publisher.

Table of Contents

Some words are shown in bold, **like this.** You can find out what they mean by looking in the glossary.

Chapter 1: Who Were the Aztecs?

The **ancestors** of the Aztecs were **hunter-gatherers**. They roamed through the deserts. They wore hides and hunted with light bows and arrows.

In the 1200s, the ancestors of the Aztecs arrived at Lake Texcoco in the Valley of Mexico. They began to claim land. Finally, the Aztec ancestors started to fight with the people who lived there before them. The Aztecs defeated the other groups and built the city of Tenochtitlán. The city was named after the ruler, Tenoch. Tenochtitlán became the capital of the Aztec **empire**.

By making war on neighboring kingdoms, the Aztecs built an **empire**. During the 1400s and early 1500s, the Aztecs ruled a large area of central and southern Mexico. The empire reached its peak in the early 1500s, under the emperor Montezuma II.

In 1519, Spanish explorer Hernan Cortés arrived. At first Montezuma welcomed him.

This picture shows the emperor Montezuma wearing traditional costume.

Timeline

1200s	1325	1502	1519	1521
Ancestors of Aztecs begin to settle in the Valley of Mexico, around Lake Texcoco.	The city of Tenochtitlán is founded.	Montezuma II becomes Aztec ruler.	Spanish explorer Hernan Cortés arrives in the Valley of Mexico.	Spanish conquer Aztec empire.

He gave him gifts and held feasts. But he soon became worried because the Spaniards were joining with neighboring kingdoms against the Aztecs. The Spaniards had better armor and weapons than the Aztecs. They were highly trained warriors.

When Montezuma heard that the Spaniards had joined his enemies, he knew his forces could not beat them in open battle. Montezuma decided his only choice was to invite the Spaniards into Tenochtitlán. But Cortés and his men tricked Montezuma and captured him. They kept Montezuma captive in his royal apartments. Other leaders and Aztec warriors attacked the Spaniards in Montezuma's palace. No one knows exactly how it happened, but Montezuma was killed at this time.

This illustration shows Montezuma greeting Cortés when he first arrived in Mexico in 1519.

A battle was fought in Tenochtitlán. The Spaniards escaped from the city at night. They attacked again in April 1521. The Aztecs fought hard, but many died in the fighting. They also died of starvation, lack of water, and disease. In August 1521, the last Aztec emperor was captured. The Aztecs were forced to give up.

Within ten years the **empire** was ruled by Spain. The Spanish **converted** the surviving Aztecs to Christianity. They also made many of the Aztecs slaves.

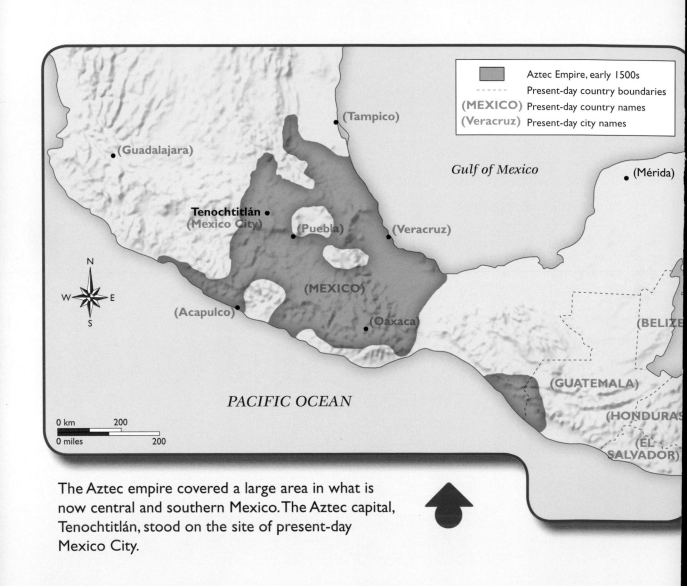

	Aztec Empire, early 1500s
- - - - -	Present-day country boundaries
(MEXICO)	Present-day country names
(Veracruz)	Present-day city names

(Tampico)

(Guadalajara)

Gulf of Mexico

(Mérida)

Tenochtitlán
(Mexico City)

(Puebla)

(Veracruz)

N
W E
S

(MEXICO)

(Acapulco)

(Oaxaca)

(BELIZE)

(GUATEMALA)

PACIFIC OCEAN

(HONDURAS)

0 km 200
0 miles 200

(EL SALVADOR)

The Aztec empire covered a large area in what is now central and southern Mexico. The Aztec capital, Tenochtitlán, stood on the site of present-day Mexico City.

Aztec art

For the Aztecs, art was connected to religion and nature. The most highly prized Aztec artists were painters. Painters created the codices, or books, that recorded all the important parts of Aztec life. Aztec painters also used their skills to decorate pottery.

Aztec artists created beautiful works of art using feathers that they collected from colorful birds such as parrots and hummingbirds. They made headdresses, shields, cloaks, fans, and clothing for rulers, warriors, and other people. Feather work was so respected that even Aztecs of the upper classes worked hard to master the craft. Aztecs admired feather work even more than goldsmithing. Gold was used to make jewelry, cups, jars, masks, and other objects.

Aztec riddle

The Aztecs were excellent poets and speakers. They loved witty sayings and riddles. Here is an example of an Aztec riddle: What is a mountainside that has a spring of water flowing in it?

Answer: Our nose.

Aztecs were master goldsmiths. This gold pendant shows an Aztec ruler dressed for a ritual. He holds a battle axe, a staff shaped like a snake, and a shield.

Aztec religion

Religion and **spiritual** beliefs were at the center of Aztec life. Aztecs believed that all parts of nature, from birds to ears of corn, to rocks and wind, were alive with spirit. Even works of art had spiritual meaning. The Sun Stone is a famous stone carving. It shows the Aztecs' view of how the world was created.

Aztecs believed that a god named Ometecuhtli, or Two Lord, and a goddess named Omecihuatl, or Two Lady, created the world. They had four sons. Each of these sons ruled over one direction—east, west, north, and south. The gods tore apart a terrifying she-monster. Out of her body came plants, rivers, valleys, and mountains. But in exchange for these gifts, she demanded human blood. The Aztec religion had many rituals that included the spilling of blood.

The Sun Stone shows the Aztecs' beliefs about the history of the world. They believed that the Earth had been created and destroyed four times and that they lived in the fifth era.

The Aztecs also worshiped a rain god, a goddess of water, fire and earth gods, plant gods, a sun god, and many others. They believed that the gods gave them life, created the world, and provided all the things the people needed to live. The power of the gods showed itself in powerful natural events such as thunder, wind, rain, and rushing rivers.

This is a sculpture of Tlaloc, the ancient god of rain.

Chapter 2: Daily Life

The Aztecs believed that every person had a place in society. Their society was divided according to rank. Some people had more power, money, and rights than others. Nobles were at the top of the Aztec social scale. Land-owning commoners were in the middle. At the bottom were farmers who worked the land of others, and slaves.

Nobles owned most of the land. They worked as warriors, clerks, judges, historians, and tax collectors. All the nobles received tribute, or payments in goods and services, from the commoners. Boys and girls of the noble class had their own schools. There they learned subjects they would need to take their place as leaders at the top of society when they grew up.

This pendant would have been worn by a nobleman or high-priest. It is made from jade.

Aztecs built small raised plots of land called *chinampas* in Lake Texcoco. They grew crops and sometimes built their homes on *chinampas*.

Some commoners owned small plots of land where they grew crops. Some of them fished for a living. Others ran small businesses. Still others did hard labor, such as building and repairing palaces and public buildings. Commoners could improve themselves by becoming skilled artists, merchants, or warriors. Children of commoners also went to school. They mostly learned job skills, the basics of warfare, and how to be a good citizen.

In times of hardship, a person or a whole family could sell themselves into slavery. Thieves and people in debt or gamblers who lost all their money might become slaves for a time. Owners did not pay slaves for their work. However, slaves were allowed to own property and were free to marry whom they wished. Slaves could make money in their spare time, and some even became rich. If a slave became rich enough, he or she could buy his or her freedom.

Home life

Aztecs saw themselves as belonging to their town or city, then their neighborhood, and finally their family. Daily life centered around the neighborhood. In most neighborhoods, people of all classes and jobs mingled. Each neighborhood had its own special god or goddess and a **temple** dedicated to it. People of the neighborhood gathered at the temple to worship.

Aztecs lived in single-family homes. A family was made up of a husband and wife and their children. Women took care of the house, and men worked outside the home. Children stayed with their parents until they married, around the age of 15 for girls and 20 for men. Children were raised with strict discipline. Parents might stick misbehaving children with thorns.

Bowls like these were made and decorated by women in the home.

Popcorn, peanuts, and lizards

The main food of the Aztecs was corn. They made corn flatbread called tortillas, as well as corn cakes and porridge. The Aztecs ate many types of beans, grains, vegetables, and fruits. Fish and meat were eaten in smaller amounts. Aztecs ate lizards, insects, and worms. They also enjoyed popcorn and peanuts.

The prickly pear cactus was one source of food for the Aztecs.

Chocolate and chili

Chocolate is made from the beans of cacao trees. These trees grew in the Valley of Mexico. The Aztecs used cacao beans to make a chocolate drink. Only the upper classes could drink chocolate because it was scarce. The drink was made by roasting and grinding cacao beans. Then the cacao powder was mixed with water. Aztecs beat the liquid with a wooden whisk and flavored it with vanilla and chili powder.

Chapter 3: Gossip and Games

Every Aztec community had a market. The market was an important social center. Officials patrolled markets to make sure all business was carried out honestly. People of all ages flocked to the marketplaces. Buying and selling was fun. It was also a place to meet and gossip with friends.

Aztec children were expected to work hard, study hard, and behave properly from a young age. Much of their time was spent learning the skills they would need as adults. But they had some time for play. Many of their toys were smaller versions of grown-up tools. Boys played with weapons, for example, and girls played with spinning and cooking utensils.

Aztec children played with toys like this pottery dog. They pulled it along on wheels.

Aztecs played *ollama* on an I-shaped ball court called a *tlachtli*. The object of the game was to use the elbows, knees, and hips to move a hard rubber ball through a stone ring.

Aztec athletes played a game called *ollama*. It was similar to soccer and basketball, but much rougher. *Ollama* was played on a ball court called a *tlachtli*, which was shaped like a capital letter I. High up on each side of the upright part of the I was a stone ring. The object of the game was to get a hard rubber ball through the ring. Players could use their elbows, knees, and hips to move the ball.

Another popular form of entertainment was playing a board game called *patolli*. *Patolli* was similar to backgammon. Players raced to be the first to move their game pieces around a board.

By doing the hands-on activities and crafts in this chapter, you'll get a feel for what life was like for the Aztecs.

Recipe: Corn Tortillas

Corn was the most important part of the Aztecs' diet. The most common item made from corn was tortillas. After you make your corn tortillas, use them to scoop up beans, or wrap them around cheese, meat, or vegetables, or any combination of these foods. Aztecs prepared corn for making tortillas by cooking corn kernels with lime to make a dough. Then they ground the dough on a flat piece of stone. They used their hands to form flat, round tortillas, just like those many people enjoy today.

Supplies and Ingredients
- Mixing bowl
- Measuring cups
- Large pan, griddle, or skillet
- Spatula
- 2 cups (500 ml) corn flour, also called masa
- Cooking oil or nonstick spray

This picture from a codex shows Aztecs eating a meal together.

Corn tortillas can be used for a variety of traditional Mexican dishes.

1 Follow the directions on the corn flour package to create dough.

❱ After making the dough, allow it to sit for five minutes. This makes the dough easier to handle.

3 Form a ball of dough about 1 inch (2.5 centimeters) in diameter.

4 Sprinkle flour on your hands to prevent sticking. Pat the ball back and forth between your hands. Pat it until it is flat and thin.

5 Coat a pan lightly with cooking oil or nonstick spray. Heat the pan on medium-high heat.

6 Place the tortilla on the pan and cook until slightly brown. Flip the tortilla with a spatula. It should take about two minutes to cook the tortilla.

❱ You can serve tortillas with cheese, beans, vegetables, or meat.

Craft: Make a Feather Headdress

Feather work was among the most highly prized Aztec art. Aztecs raised birds for their feathers. Hunters also caught birds in the forests. Feather workers might tie the shafts, or bare ends, of the feathers into cloth while it was being woven. Or they glued or tied feathers to a base of cotton or a stiff leaf. Warriors, priests, nobles, and rulers wore feather ornaments and clothing at important ceremonies and festivals. Commoners were not allowed to wear feather items.

Warning!

Make sure to read all of the directions before beginning the project.

Feather work was very important to the Aztecs. You should treat your headdress with dignity and respect.

This is a feathered headdress that historians believe Montezuma gave to Cortés. Montezuma's own headdress was made of 400 feathers of the quetzal bird.

Supplies:

- Posterboard or stiff paper cut to 24 inches by 2 inches. (Option: use craft leather available at hobby stores, cut to size.)
- Pencil
- Scissors
- Stapler or tape
- Glue
- Sequins, glitter, foil
- Feathers (available at craft stores) or construction paper cut into feather shapes
- Crayons or markers

1 Your posterboard will be the headband. Use a pencil to create a design or pattern on your posterboard, . This may be shapes and lines, or an illustration of a story. For example, you could illustrate various animals or gods that were important to the Aztecs, such as jaguars or the feathered serpent.

2 Use crayons or markers to color your design or illustration. You can also glue sequins, or glitter, or foil onto the headband.

3 Glue, staple, or tape the feathers onto the back of the headband so they poke out along the top. Make a pattern from different colors or shapes of feathers. (See Picture A)

A

4 Have someone wrap the headband around your head so the two ends overlap at the back of your head. Have them use a pencil to mark the spot on the headband where one end overlaps the other. (See Picture B)

B

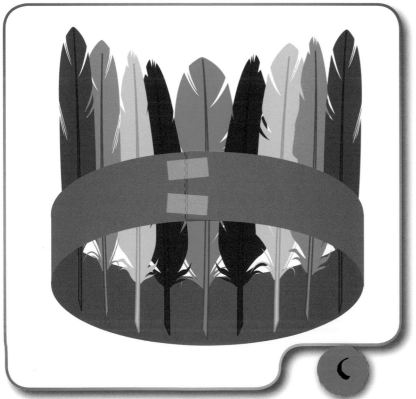

C

5 Take the headband off of your head and overlap the ends so that they match the mark that was made. Use tape or a stapler to fasten the headband, so it stays in a circle. (See Picture C)

Feather Headdress

You can make your feather
headdress in any combination
of colors.

Can you explain the
illustrations you drew?
Does the pattern of the
feathers have a special
meaning for you?

Craft: Make a Codex

Aztec artists recorded important information about their world and their beliefs in codices. Codices were kept by wise teachers called *tlamatinime*, or "knowers of things." The illustrations in the codices look a little like cartoons. They show pictures of gods and goddesses, animals, and symbols representing calendar points and points in the sky. The codices were made from the bark of the fig tree, or from animal hide. They were folded back and forth, like a fan.

Warning!
Read all directions before beginning the project.

Supplies:
- 1 piece of 6-inch by 18-inch drawing or construction paper
  (any long piece of paper will work, the cover should be 1/4 inch taller and wider than the book)
- 2 pieces of 6 ¼ by 4 ¾ inch posterboard, cardboard, railroad board, or oakboard
- 24 inches of string or yarn
- Glue or glue stick

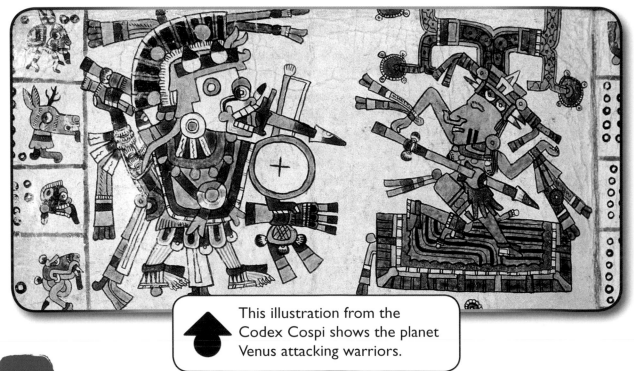

This illustration from the Codex Cospi shows the planet Venus attacking warriors.

1 Place the paper in front of you, horizontally.

2 Fold it in half down the middle. (See Picture A)

3 Fold the top page in half by folding it back to meet the first fold. (See Picture B)

4 Turn the paper over and repeat this process, folding the top page back to meet the first fold.

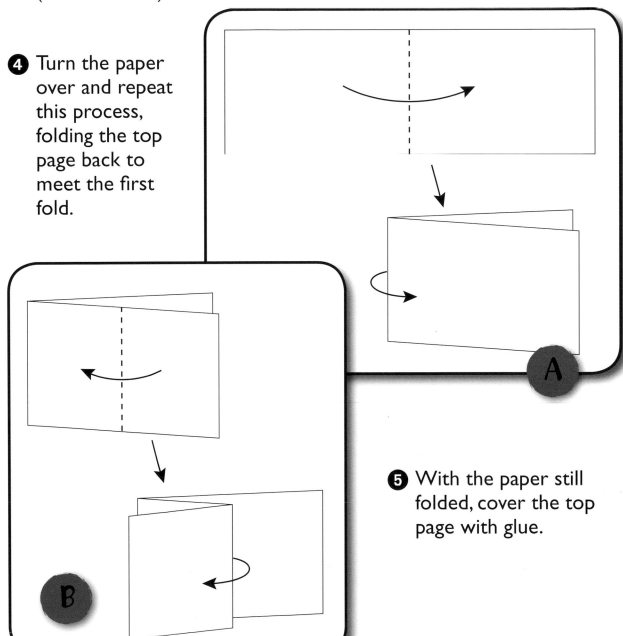

5 With the paper still folded, cover the top page with glue.

6 Place one posterboard piece face down in front of you. Carefully pick up the folded bunch of paper, and glue the top page down to the posterboard. Make sure it is centered and even. (See Picture C)

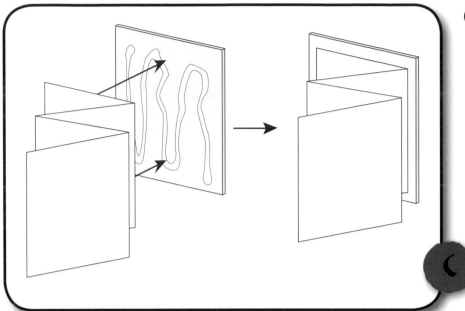

7 Now, with the last page of the folded paper facing up, cover it with glue.

8 Repeat the process of placing the other piece of posterboard in front of you, and carefully gluing the last page down to it. Check to make sure it lines up with the other posterboard cover.

9 Lay the string across the back of the book, from side to side. Make sure that the ends of the string are even.

10 Wrap the string around the book and tie it across the front in a bow.

11 Turn the book back over and glue the ribbon in place. (See Picture D)

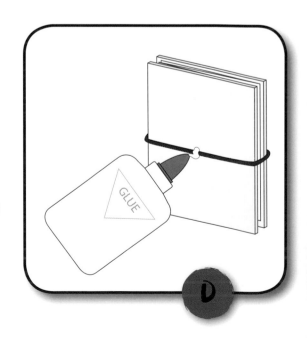

12 When you want to write in your book, untie the string and lay the book down on its back.

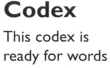

Will you use the codex for drawings or words?

Codex

This codex is ready for words and drawings.

FOR MORE PAGES IN YOUR BOOK

Before adding the back cover, take a second piece of long paper and fold it like you did with the first one. Glue this set of pages to the last page in your first set. Then glue the back cover to the last page of the second set. You can also make more pages by making each one smaller. Instead of folding the long paper in half, try folding it into thirds, then folding each third in half.

Craft: Make a Patolli Board

A *patolli* board was like a big X divided into squares. The players threw beans that worked like dice. The winner was the player who was the first to move his or her six pebbles from the beginning to the end of the board. The game often drew crowds of spectators. People would bet on the outcome. They could win or lose valuable goods. In fact, there are records of people losing everything they owned on *patolli* games and having to sell themselves into slavery.

Aztecs played *patolli* on an X-shaped board.

Supplies:
- Posterboard or large drawing paper, about 24 inches by 36 inches
- Pencil
- Drawing paper or construction paper (optional)
- Ruler or yardstick
- Markers, crayons, or paint
- 7 dried beans or 1 dice and 2 playing pieces

26

◗ Use a pencil to draw a large "X" or cross shape on the posterboard. Make it big: each arm of the "X" or cross should be about two or three inches wide, and long enough to reach almost from one end of the posterboard to the other. Use a ruler or yardstick to make straight lines. This is your *patolli* game board.

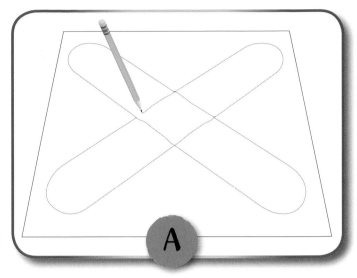

A

◗ There are four arms to the *patolli* board. Draw lines across the arms where they meet in the middle. This will make a box in the middle. (See Picture A)

❸ Draw across each arm of the *patolli* board so that you divide each arm into three equal sections. (See Picture B)

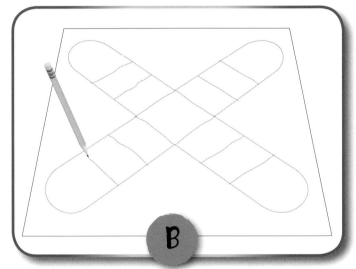

B

❹ Draw a line from the box down the middle of each arm to its end. You'll be drawing four lines in all. (See Picture C)

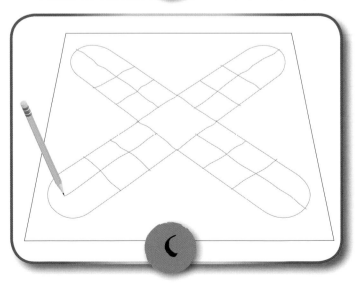

C

5 Now each arm has six sections. Look at the box in the middle of the *patolli* board. Draw a line from one corner of the box to the opposite corner. Repeat this so that you have drawn an "X" in the box.

6 The "X" that you just made divides the box into four triangles. Each triangle is now the seventh section of each arm of the *patolli* board.

7 Make a blue circle in the end section of one arm. Make a blue crown at the end of the opposite arm. (See Picture D)

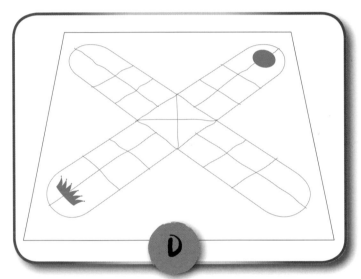

D

8 Repeat this process with green, making a green circle at one end and a green crown at the end of the last arm.

9 Pick eight empty sections on the *patolli* board at random. Draw jaguar heads in each of the eight sections. Pick another eight empty sections and draw eight marigold flowers. If you like, you can draw the jaguars and marigolds on different paper, cut them out, and glue them on the *patolli* board. You could even cut out pictures of jaguars and marigolds from magazines.

10 Use two dried beans to make playing pieces or markers. Color one of the beans blue and the other one green.

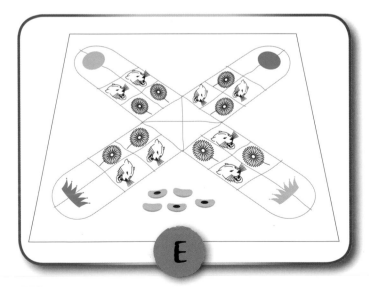

E

⓫ Make a dot on each of your remaining five beans. The beans serve as your dice. When you throw the beans, count how many land with a dot showing. This will tell you how many spaces to move when you play *patolli*. (See Picture E)

How to Play

Start each game piece on the circle of the same color. The goal is to move your piece down the board to the crown of the same color, and back to the beginning. Roll the beans or dice to determine how many spaces to move when it's your turn. If you land on a jaguar, you lose a turn. If you land on a marigold, you get an extra turn.

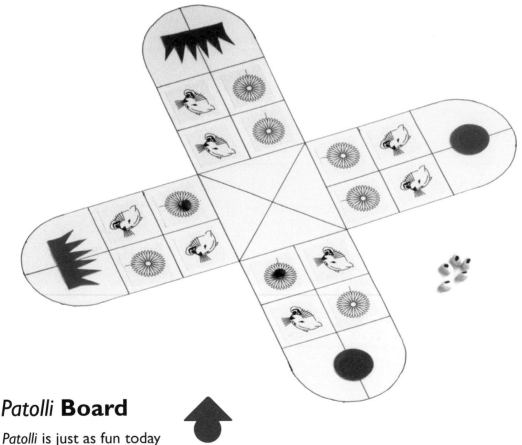

Patolli **Board**

Patolli is just as fun today as it was 500 years ago.

What other decorations can you add to your game board?

Glossary

ancestor person who is a relative from an earlier time. For example, grandparents, great-grandparents, and great-great grandparents are ancestors

convert change a person from one set of beliefs to another, sometimes by force

empire group of countries ruled by a single country or ruler

hunter-gatherer person who gets food by hunting animals and collecting foods such as fruits, roots, plants, nuts, and other things that grow naturally

spiritual things that have to do with people's souls rather than their bodies

temple place where holy objects are kept and where people go to pray

More Books To Read

Allan, Tony. *The Aztec Empire* (*Excavating the Past* series). Chicago: Heinemann, 2004.

Jovinelly, Joann. *The Crafts and Culture of the Aztecs.* New York: Rosen, 2002.

Wood, Marion. *Growing up in Aztec Times.* Mahwah, NJ: Troll Communications, 2003.

Wyborny, Sheila. *Life During the Aztec Empire.* Farmington Hills, MI: Gale Group, 2003.

The instructions for these projects are designed to allow students to work as independently as possible. However, it is always a good idea to make a prototype before assigning any project so that students can see how their own work will look when completed. Prior to introducing these projects, teachers should collect and prepare the materials and be ready for any modifications that may be necessary. Participating in the project-making process will help teachers understand the directions and be ready to assist students with difficult steps. Teachers might also choose to adapt or modify the projects to better suit the needs of an individual student or class. No one knows what levels of achievement students will reach better than their teacher.

While it is preferable for students to work as independently as possible, there is some flexibility in regards to project materials and tools. They can vary according to what is available. For instance, while standard white glue may be most familiar to students, there might be times when a teacher will choose to speed up a project by using a hot glue gun to fasten materials for students. Likewise, while a project may call for leather cord, it is feasible in most instances to substitute vinyl cord or even yarn or rope. Acrylic paint may be recommended because it adheres better to a material like felt or plastic, but other types of paint would be suitable as well. Circles can be drawn with a compass, or simply by tracing a cup, roll of tape, or other circular object. Allowing students a broad spectrum of creativity and opportunities to problem-solve within the parameters of a given project will encourage their critical thinking skills most fully.

Each project contains an italicized question somewhere in the directions. These questions are meant to be thought-provoking and promote discussion while students work on the project.

Index